A MODERN MILIEU

A Modern Milieu
Julius Meier-Graefe

Edited and with an Epilogue by Markus Breitschmid

Translated by Harry Francis Mallgrave
and Markus Breitschmid

Virginia Tech Architecture Publications

A Modern Milieu
Julius Meier-Graefe
Volume 1 of Series *Texts on Architecture & Art*

Editor: Markus Breitschmid
Translation from German to English: Harry Francis Mallgrave & Markus Breitschmid
Epilogue / Biographical Text: Markus Breitschmid
Layout: Allison Drucker
Corrector of Epilogue: Brittani Morris

Originally published in German as:
Title: Ein modernes Milieu
Author: Julius Meier-Graefe
In: Dekorative Kunst Volume 8 / No. 7. Munich IV / 1901, pp. 249-264.

Virginia Tech Architecture Publications
Blacksburg, Virginia 24061-0205
United States of America
Phone: +1-540-231-5383
Internet: www.archdesign.vt.edu

Printed in the United States of America

Texts on Architecture & Art Series

The intent of the series 'Texts on Architecture & Art' is to make important texts on architecture and art originally published in other languages available to an English-speaking readership. Each volume consists of a first-time English translation of a text on architecture or art. The series is dedicated to the understanding of theoretical problems of architecture and art.

Series Editor: Markus Breitschmid

A Modern Milieu

The original edition of the text presented in this volume is titled *Ein Modernes Milieu*. The text was written by Julius Meier-Graefe in Paris. It was originally published in the art magazine *Dekorative Kunst* in 1901.

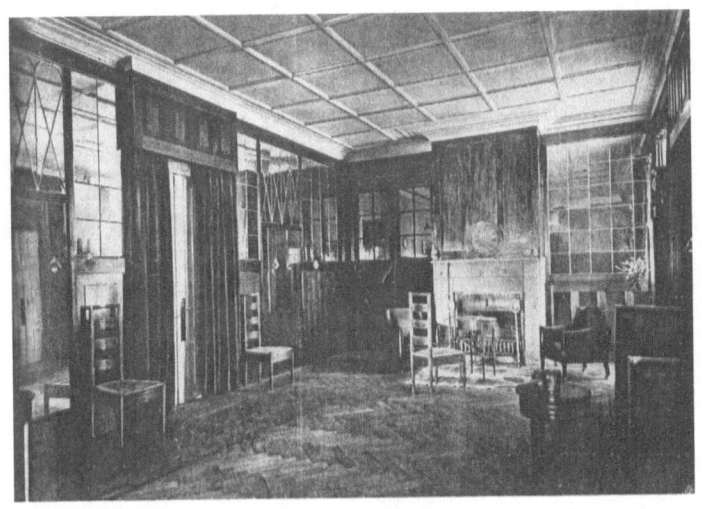

ENTRANCE HALL. R.A. SCHRÖDER WITH ARCHITECT MARTIN DÜLFER WITH THE COOPERATION OF P. TROOST

It is very awkward to use two foreign terms in a title of three words, but nothing else comes to my mind for what I would like to describe. It concerns an apartment, of which dozens have been discussed in these pages over the course of this year; for this particular apartment a more generally accepted expression does not suit. I struggle with the description like the critics did with the first impressionists. They preferred the term "picture" because "painting" was not good enough, despite the fact that the thing remained the same in principle. Even the painters themselves scratched their heads to find new titles.

In principle, every apartment is a milieu as soon as someone lives in it. The difference lies in what the impressionist painters believed to have been their invention: atmosphere in the sense of ambience. Germans have made do with apartments without ambience for several decades, and even today millions are stuck in an existence without perspective. They move in and out without leaving behind a trace. The structure of the big city—the rational principle of rental units that strives to turn a room into a cabin of a sleeping car—is helping. Enterprising architects are doing their part.

One can have ambience in a truly dreadful apartment. Our elders have shown this. They lived without a clue, without an inkling of the decorative renaissance with which their sons dressed themselves. And how homey did they have it! Who—in unobserved moments away from the impersonal splendor and rational logic of all the artistic rules of a Modern apartment—does not long to return to the quiet abomination of the good old living room!

We begin to occupy modern apartments, only we still lack the people for it. We lack the people who understand how to make Modern things their own, people who are able to take away the always awkward newness from the new, people who are able to conduct themselves appropriately in the new style, people who bring life to it—ambience.

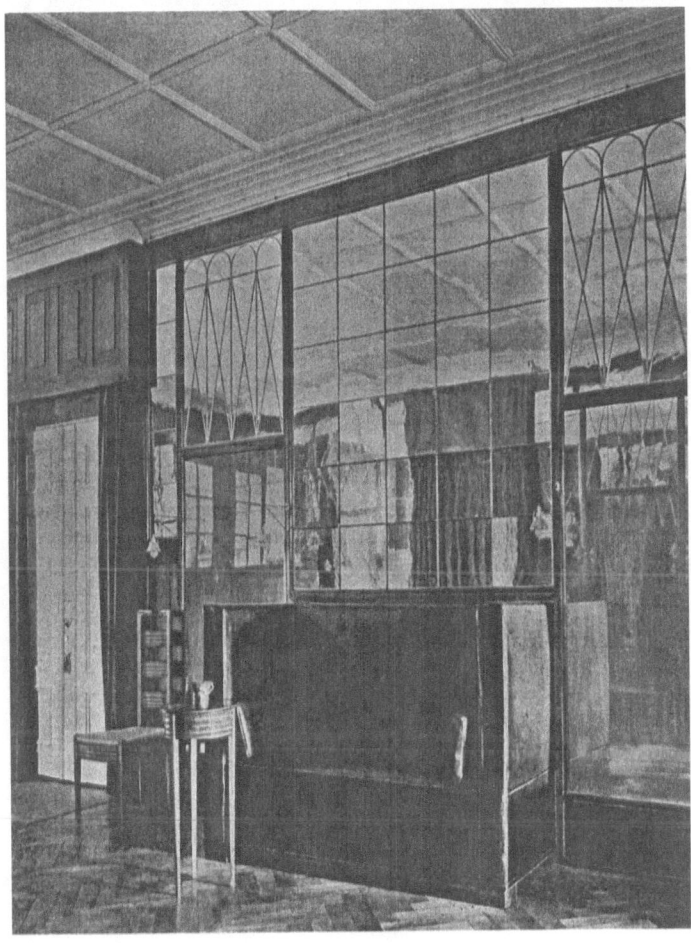

WALL OF ENTRANCE HALL. R.A. SCHRÖDER WITH M. DÜLFER AND P. TROOST

Two things characterize it: certain qualities of the dwelling and certain qualities of the inhabitant. We should be honest enough to admit that what is Modern does not always make it easy for inhabitants to express these qualities. There are, for instance, things in Modern decoration that are absolutely without a context, because they were conceived outside the realm of the spirit of the likeable inhabitant. They exhibit a more or less penetrating originality and at best they are suited for today's not to be neglected purpose of being depicted in art journals. All of this was and is just fine, because in this world even the simplest things cannot be achieved without a struggle. These decorative symptoms were the banners of war in the struggle, and if they should be put aside in due time one should even hang them with laurels twice. It was not possible to fight the old ornament with cool logic but it had to be done with new ornament— although one does not need ornament for salvation. The all-too human being demands that we place less emphasis on actual purpose. We had to give the world examples of our enormous originality in order to shed ourselves from it more confidently afterwards. What spirited youth, in his first ball

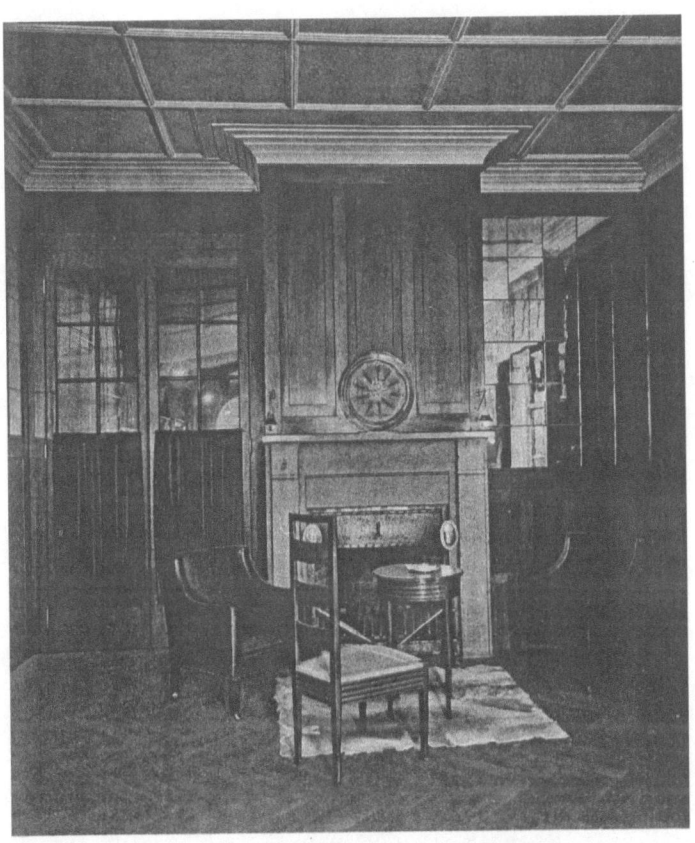

FIREPLACE IN ENTRANCE HALL. R.A. SCHRÖDER WITH M. DÜLFER AND P. TROOST

season, does not succumb to the temptation of making a poet out of his tailor by wearing intoxicating waistcoats and tails! If someone older still attempts to express his personality in this cheerful frippery, he can easily become slightly ludicrous, even if his inner demeanor is serious. Thus the person upon growing older will normally feel the pressure to become anonymous and conceal his individuality—if he possesses it—under the most harmless cover. One may keep the strong desire to wear perfectly fitted cloth, but only in the most discreet fabrics.

This wish must necessarily carry over into the question of apartments. The milieu may be just as simple if it fits, and theory—whether it belongs to this or that evolution of Modern architecture and Modern painting—will gravitate toward the more natural question of whether the milieu corresponds well with the loving self.

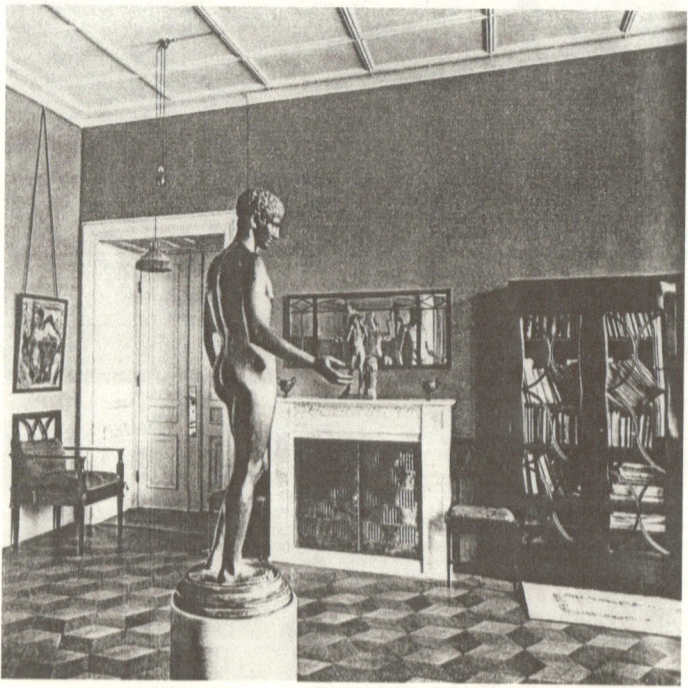

LIBRARY AND RECEPTION ROOM R.A. R.A. Schröder with M. Dülfer and P. TROOST. MANUFACTURED IN DARK MOHOGANY BY THE VEREINIGTE WERKSTÄTEN FOR ART AND CRAFT, MUNICH.

Neither VAN DE VELDE nor ECKMANN, nor PLUMET, nor anyone else has thought about this. Every apartment became a new stone of their crown; they put their own personality in their designs, not that of their clients. The rooms say nothing of them and this has not necessarily to do with the fact that the clients have nothing to say. The designers did not know them. If nobody would expect a suit without a fitting from a tailor, we should not expect a harmonious result between an artist and his client without a personal relationship. With the commission of an apartment the measuring is confined to the weighing of the purse. To be sure the client still expresses his wish in the selection of the wood. In young cultural states like Berlin one takes care to limit such advice to a single opinion, and by the way they are pretty good and wise in doing that.

The apartment about which I will speak has above all the advantage of being lived in, that is, of being created to a certain extent out of instincts. In theory instincts are also present in our artists, but exercised more as a general principle than as a personal object. And they are overcome by subjective tendencies.

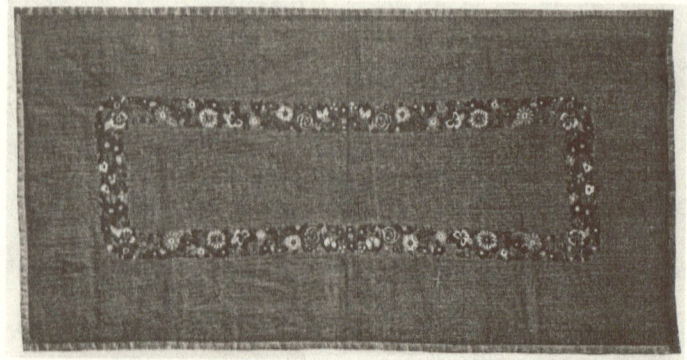

Hand-Embroidered Carpet (Grospoint). Designed by R.A. Schröder, Details by H. Vogeler, Worpswede

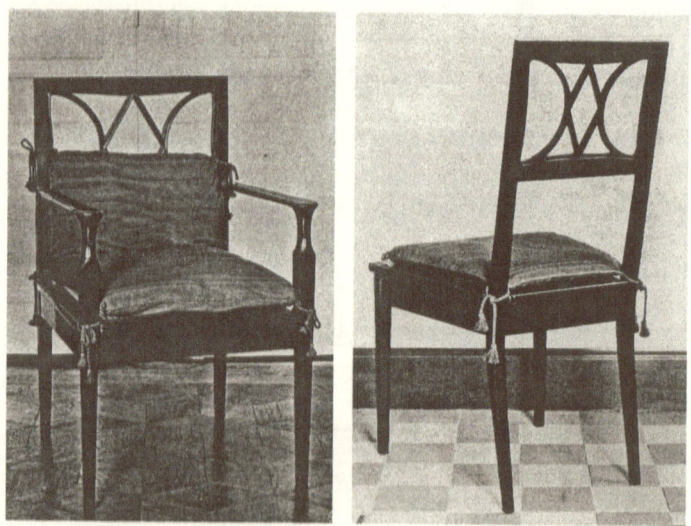

Chairs. Manufactured by the *Vereinigte Werkstätten*, Munich

The apartment is located in Munich and has been designed by RUDOLF ALEXANDER SCHRÖDER for his cousin, ALFRED WALTER HEYMEL. Both men, together with OTTO JULIUS BIERBAUM, are publishers of the collaboratively edited journal *Die Insel*.

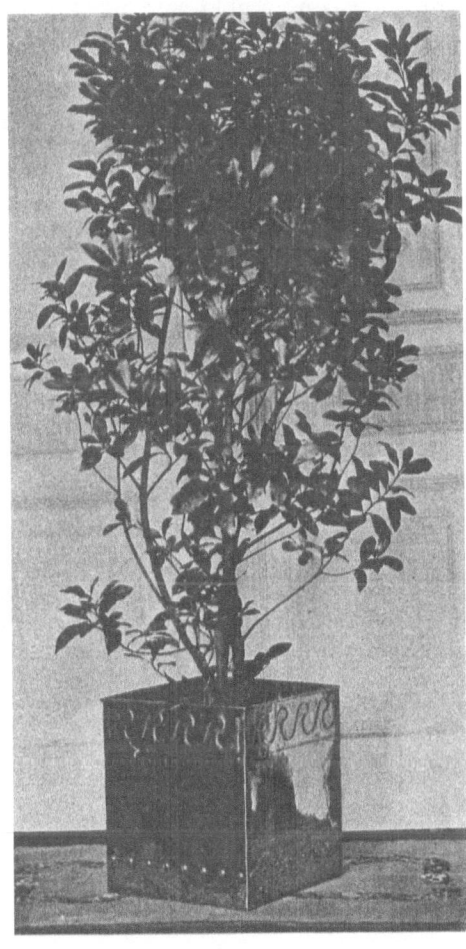

FLOWER POT IN BRASS. MANUFACTURED BY STEINICKEN & LOHR, MUNICH

We have genuinely original people in all arts. What we still need in poetry, painting, sculpture, and architecture is the mastery of taste.

Taste is especially typical in the HEYMEL apartment. It manifests itself most assuredly in the tendency, before all else, to create something comfortable, and to be sure something comfortable for a specific person. Both friends are so close that SCHRÖDER just had to let himself be himself in order to fulfill his task. He did this with the self-assurance of a very harmonious man, in whom need takes no notice of a self-indulgent exterior. With no pretension but with the unconscious logic of his manner he stamps everything he handles, everything worthwhile. The remarkable thing about this apartment is the absence of all dilettantism. It is exactly what the dilettante is most impressed with of the Modern — the new ornament — that is avoided here with cool assurance. Rarely has any artist achieved this. The sensible insight of not doing something, for which a special talent is required if the design should be original — this generally so very lacking insight is usually replaced by superficial imitation. Here it leads to a solution of almost programmatic effects.

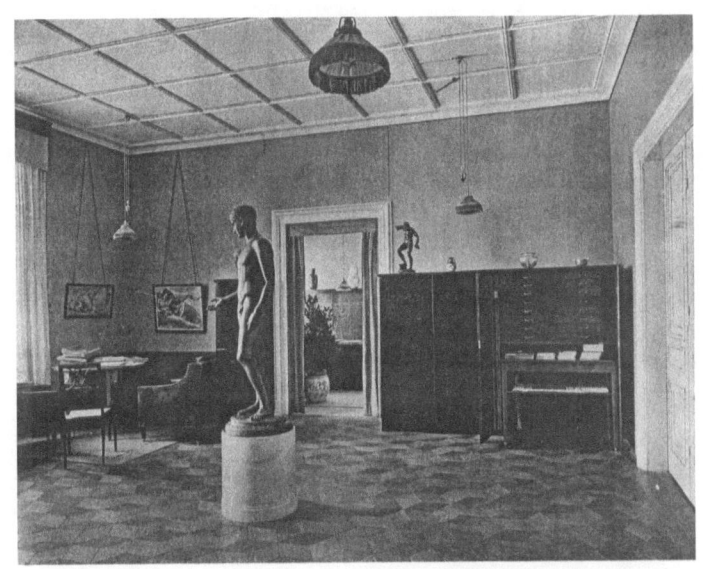

LIBRARY AND RECEPTION ROOM. R.A. SCHRÖDER WITH M. DÜLFER AND P. TROOST

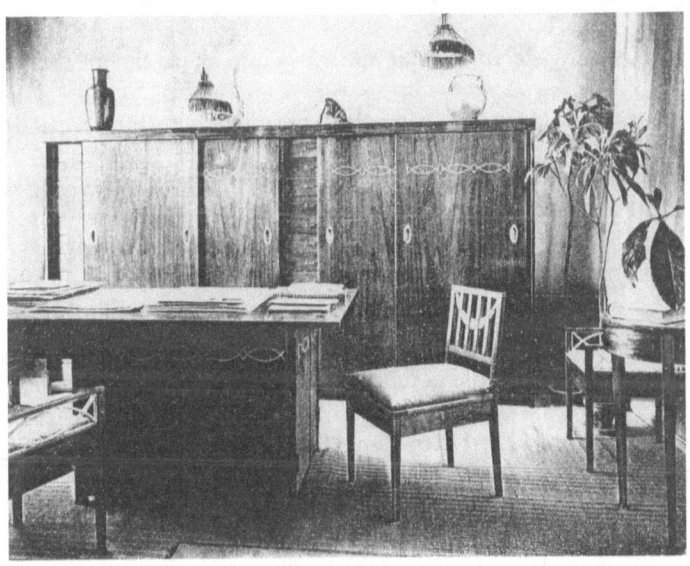

COPPERPLATE CABINET. R.A. SCHRÖDER WITH M. DÜLFER AND P. TROOST. MANUFACTURED IN LIGHT MAHOGANY BY THE *VEREINIGTE WERSTÄTTEN*, MUNICH

19

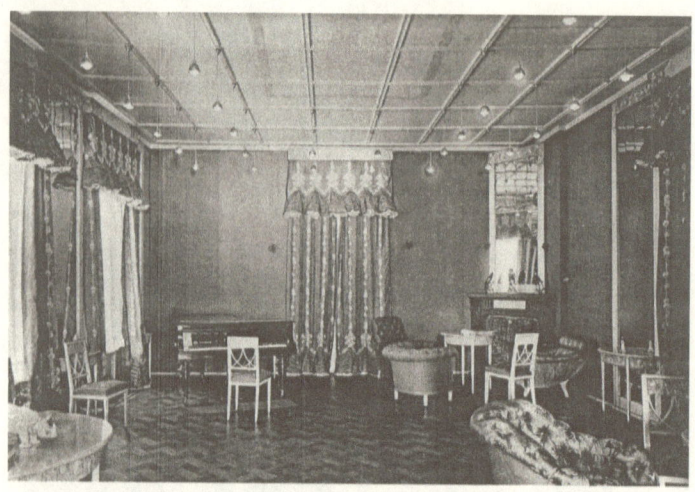

SALON. R.A. SCHRÖDER WITH M. DÜLFER AND P. TROOST. MANUFACTURED IN WHITE-PAINTED WOOD BY THE *VEREINIGTE WERKSTÄTTEN* FOR ART AND CRAFT, MUNICH

Nowhere does one find the famed Belgian line that already decorates the barbershops of east Prussian villages. There is scarcely any decoration at all. Here and there the artist felt it necessary to introduce a splash of color, something ruffled, something wide or long. How this splash is detailed was less important to the artist. He prefers beautiful stylized flowers or is pleased with a wreath of leaves reduced to a minimum, or he selects a simple geometric ornament. With the greatest ease he has returned to the tenet that ornament is only a detail and has to disappear in the whole. Yet for this whole, as it presents itself in the principal lines and surfaces, SCHRÖDER took the greatest care. He had to work with a large rental

20

apartment with all of the numerous clichés of the Modern tenement style. No ceiling or door could remain in place. He gave his greatest attention to the walls; he did not have to deal with a client who was concerned with the temporary nature of the rental apartment. He was allowed to spend the bulk of the budget that would be lost in a move to another apartment.

Exactly here we see the noble sensitivity of the client as well as of the artist. It rules in the almost antediluvian soundness of the rooms, just as we find it in the old patrician houses of our Hanseatic cities. As a matter of fact, SCHRÖDER and HEYMEL are from Bremen. The most essential part of the furniture is built into the walls, not in complicated forms but in a simple and practical way. Principally because of the few pieces of furniture, the rooms have only so much as is necessary to structure them. No trifles — the seats are of a vast size; next to them chairs, even English leather rocking chairs, appear like dwarfs. There are numerous sofas, everyone almost as deep as long; there is no visible wood in the seats, not even the smallest cheap attempt at carving a flourish. It would appear clumsy if it were not well arranged.

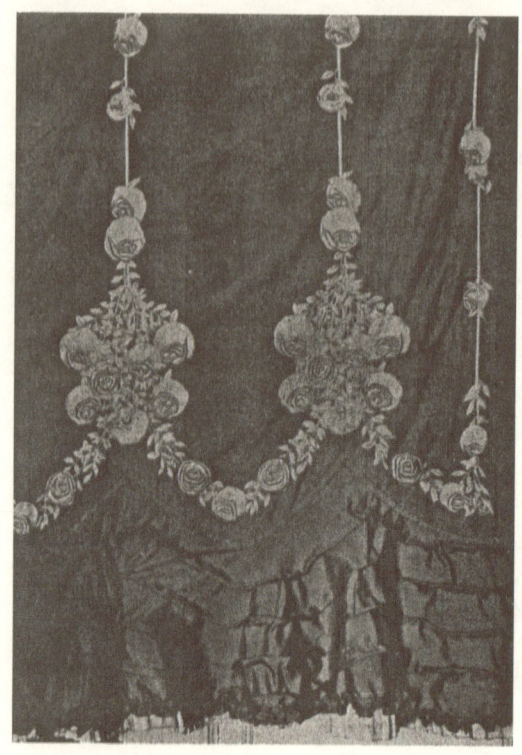

DETAIL OF CURTAIN IN SALON

And precisely in this lies its greatest charm: this weighty simplicity does not lack grace. Small round tables stand in front of the giant sofas; the large closets are ingeniously divided. Materials change with astounding assurance.

Take the bedroom, for example. The bed is enormous, an authentic Nordic construction as wide as it is long, with a colossal canopy made entirely of heavy wood.

If everything in this room had equal weight, the room would undoubtedly feel oppressive. But the heavy fullness of the bed is playfully juxtaposed with the large sink, which is simply and elegantly made with a marble plate resting on brass legs. This purest expression of the Modern is not without audacity, for between the tall bedposts is placed a decoration that in principal does not fit: heavy, silver-plated wreaths that strongly recall the Empire. And yet it fits — a feat is pulled off.

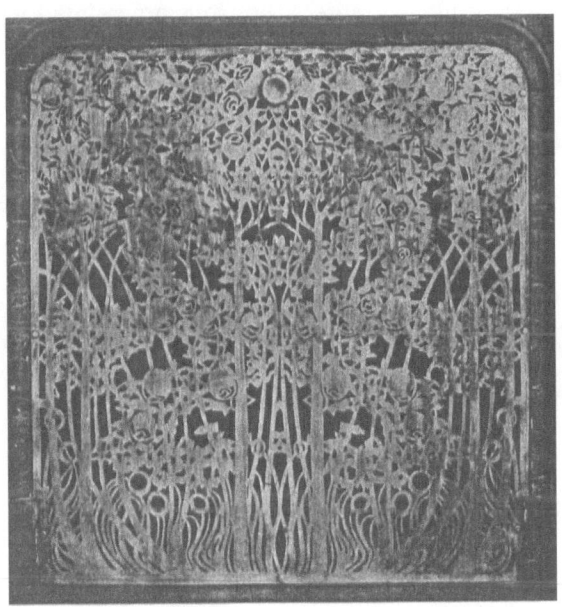

LATTICEWORK OF RADIATOR PANELING IN SALON. DESIGNED BY H. VOGELER, WORPSWEDE. MANUFACTURED WITH SILVER-PLATED COPPER BY THE *VEREINIGTE WERKSTÄTTEN*, MUNICH

In general the secret of grace amid all the heaviness lies in the happy mixing of decoration almost approaching pathos with the most temperate basic forms. The English has already shown this; here it is achieved with greater freedom. And then the colors help the lightness. The walls of the bedroom are covered with a blue silk, and conclude in a frieze of unstained mahogany. Between the bedposts and beside the windows and doors hang heavy yellow-silk curtains embroidered with large flowers in fresh colors. The dining room has brilliant colors. The walls are painted in tender pink; the floor has gray tiles without a carpet, and again there is natural mahogany. There is nothing in this large room other than the giant round table and many large chairs with straw seats—except for two narrow tables along the wall to the office. There is, in addition, much silver. Illumination is only by candles: some are placed in simple silver-plated holders on the walls, some in low candelabra on the tables. This room is also strictly stylized. The favored simple pattern of tulips can be found everywhere: in the paneling, in the chimney marble, in the damask, in the silverware, and so forth. The table spread of HEYMEL is a small

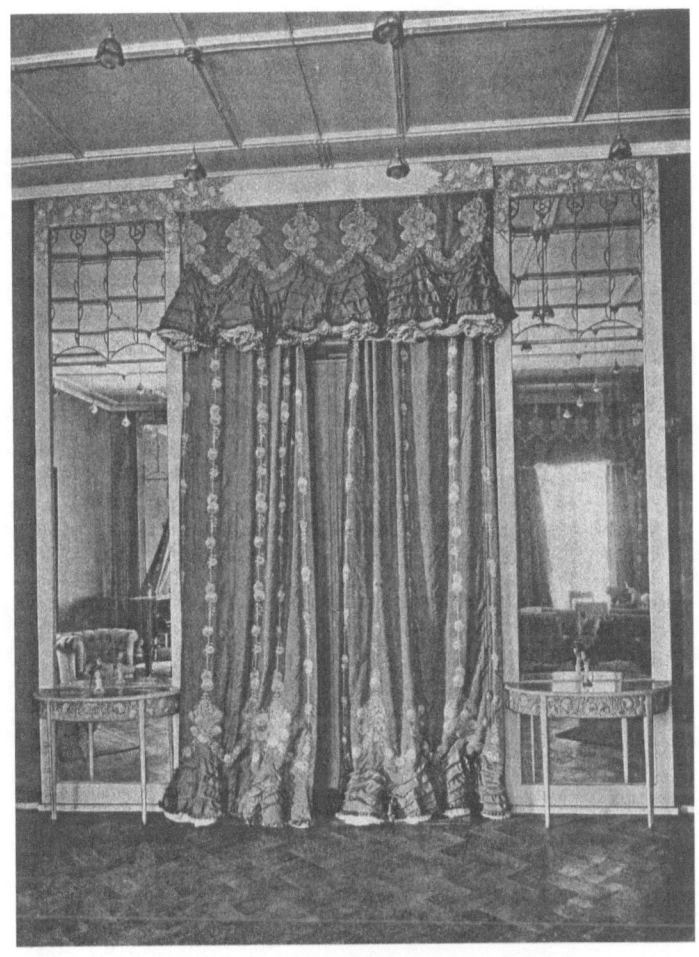

miracle of taste in precious simplicity. The silverware, which

has been tastefully and solidly designed by the Worpsweder

Vogeler, has its excellent grip inspired by a tulip bud. In

addition there are tulip glasses by Powell & Sons, and finally the porcelain: astonishingly beautiful in its simplicity, snow-white with a conscious frieze along the edge. Everything that together appears princely is individually nothing more than good bourgeoisie prosperity.

The hall is also very beautiful. It is a very large room that is entirely draped with mirrors, thinly divided with geometric lines scarcely noticeable on the surface. Here a dark, almost mystical stillness rules: nothing but these divided mirrors and large sofas with the tiny tables before them. The enormous chimney gives a very determined dignified character. In the evening, when wood is burning in the chimney and is the sole source of light, the room becomes homey. One shifts the easy-chair near to the chimney and forgets place and time: an ideal room for dreaming!

Next to the hall is the office of the *Insel*, a simple but practically furnished workroom, followed by the pearl of the whole, the grand salon. Here, again with the simplest means, one became daring. The wood is lacquered in white with carved dull-green and red roses. It is the sweetest thing imaginable, yet dyed-in-the-wool modernists will not believe that it does not have a sweet effect. From the ceiling,

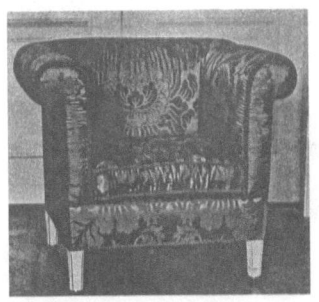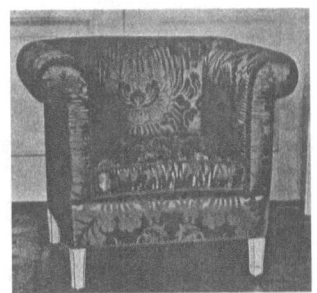

UPHOLSTERED ARM CHAIRS FOR THE SALON. SUPPLIED BY L. BERNHEIMER, MUNICH

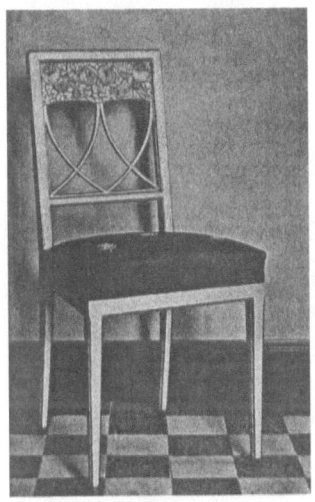

CHAIR FOR THE SALON. WITH CARVINGS,
PAINTED WHITE WITH RED CONTOURS

arranged in two large rectangles, hang almost a hundred electric lamps on cords with simple silver shades. They are decorated again with the sweetest garland of roses. The walls are covered with a gray silk approaching matte pink; sumptuous curtains of heavy silk in the same color, splendidly embroidered with white roses, dress the doors and windows, between which rises a large console mirror. The curtains are delightful. They end in puffed ruffles, from under which appear multiple white linings. One imagines that the slender feet of Colombine hiding behind each curtain, draped in white silk like a Pierrot. It is the room for beautiful women, dance, and laughter. Only in tails can one feel comfortable among the sumptuous gowns.

Typical for the taste of the two friends are the dead accessories of this room. In the corners are birds from Meissen in strong green, blue, and red colors. On the tables, around which seats of every possible form and color are grouped, we find magnificent white porcelain animals by BING & GRÖNDAHL, among which are dazzling old-roman glasses. And it is not the expensiveness of these knick-knacks that give them charm, but their seemingly nonchalant and arbitrary selection. That these things are expensive is almost incidental; this unity is achieved in other rooms with dirt-cheap vases and other things, simply through their forms and tone values.

There is not enough space to describe the other rooms. One would not gain much from it because one would have to see them. Yet there is a very distinguished copperplate

28

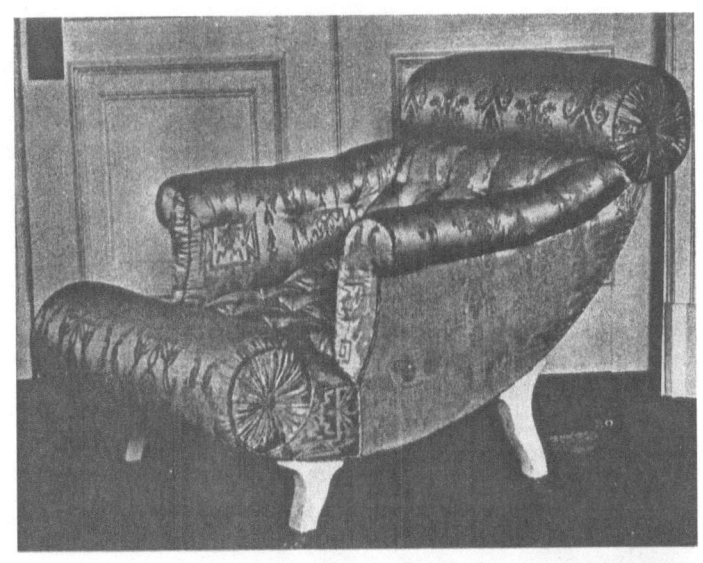

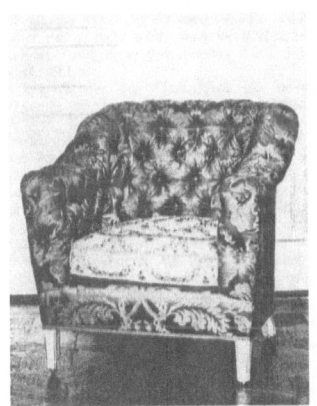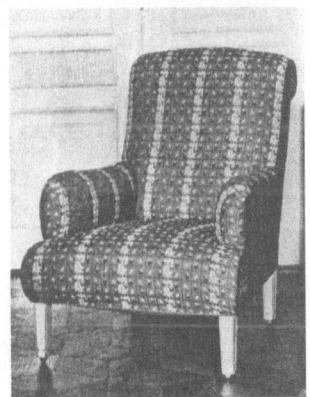

UPHOLSTERED ARM CHAIRS FOR SALON. SUPPLIED BY L. BERNHEIMER, MUNICH

cabinet kept in bright blue and walnut, with magnificent and

exceedingly practical compartments that contain drawers for

plates in the upper part and disappearing tables for rolling

out works in the lower part. There is also a billiard salon and a game room with a very suggestive bar cabinet, and a quiet homey workroom of faultless execution, mainly made by the *Vereinigte Werkstätten*. Everywhere there is the same principle of good taste and a healthy dose of common sense. This is the abiding impression and it has a salient cultural significance. Here we see that it does not require infinitely profound art or much of a Modernism *a tout-prix* to create a suitable milieu, as the prestige of most of the leading artists of our movement

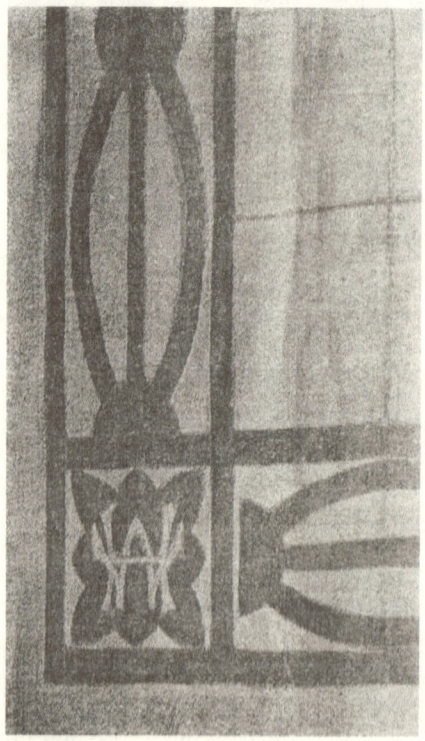

WOVEN PATTERN OF THE TABLE CLOTHS AND NAPKINS. SUPPLIED BY ROMAN MAYR, MUNICH

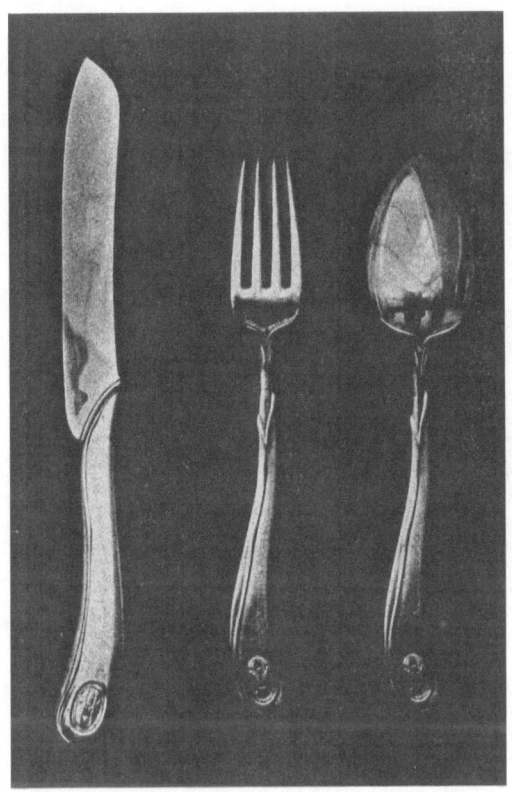

CUTLERY IN SILVER. DESIGNED BY H. VOGELER, WORPSWEDE.
MANUFACTURED BY M.H. WILCKENS & SONS, BREMEN

would like us to believe. Without exception all of them
could learn a lot from this simple solution, especially the
best of the Modern principles — that one cannot use too little
art in order to be an artist. The movement will probably
and hopefully follow SCHRÖDER's path; certainly the masses
will not. The masses will always be more impressed by the

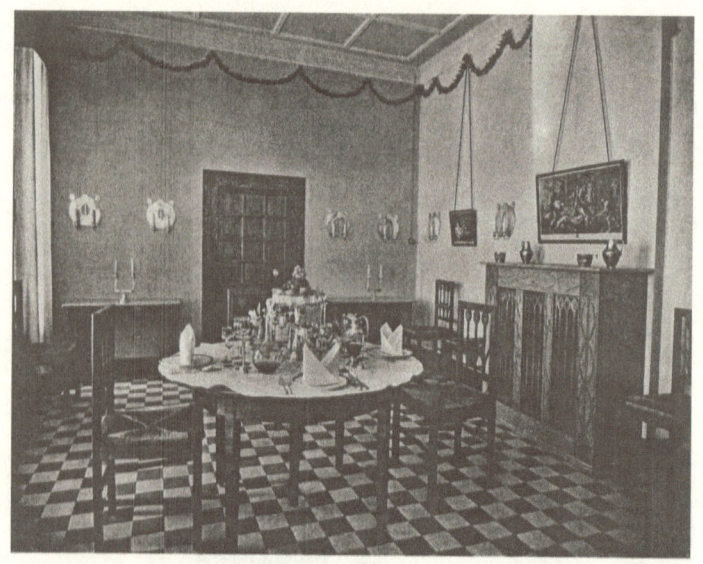

DINING ROOM. R.A. SCHRÖDER WITH M. DÜLFER AND P. TROOST. MANUFACTURED IN LIGHT MAHOGANY BY THE *VEREINIGTE WERKSTÄTTEN*, MUNICH

worst decorated thing than by the best undecorated thing. But we should expect this tendency from our leaders. The Viennese have already begun; in Vienna LOOS defiantly makes furniture without ornament and he is not without influence. In their most recent furniture MOSER and HOFFMANN display a very pleasing austerity. ECKMANN in Germany has for a long time had the same principle in his best pieces and VAN DE VELDE seems also to be turning this way, as far as his character allows. The better architects of Germany and England eagerly follow the same path, which has already become a tradition in England. It is the

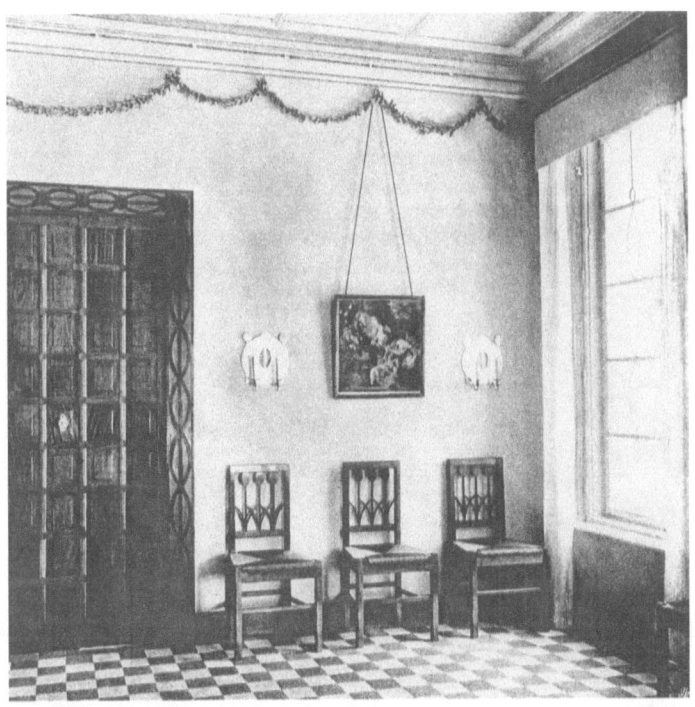

DINING ROOM. R. A. SCHRÖDER WITH M. DÜLFER AND P. TROOST

only path that will have a good influence on the craftsman.

Art lies in that which will surely protect him from dryness,

as is successfully the case with SCHRÖDER.

Ein Modernes Milieu

The following text is the original German version by Julius Meier-Graefe. It was published in the art-magazine *Dekorative Kunst* in 1901 (here printed without illustrations).

Es ist sehr misslich, in einer Überschrift von drei Worten zwei Fremdwörter zu verwenden, aber für das, was ich beschreiben möchte, fällt mir nichts anderes ein. Es handelt sich um eine Wohnung, es sind deren in diesen Blättern im Laufe der Jahre schon Duzende beschrieben worden; auf die vorliegende will der allgemeine Ausdruck nicht passen. Er geht mir damit, wie es den Kritikern mit den ersten Impressionisten erging, die Bezeichnung Bild, Gemälde war ihnen nicht genug, trotzdem im Prinzip die Sache dieselbe geblieben, und die Maler zerbrachen sich damals die Köpfe nach neuen Titeln.

Im Prinzip ist jede Wohnung ein Milieu, sobald nur jemand darin wohnt; der Unterschied liegt in dem, was in der Malerei die Impressionisten als ihre Schöpfung bezeichnen zu können glauben, in der Atmosphäre. Der

Deutsche hat mehrere Jahrzehnte sich in seiner Wohnung ohne Atmosphäre beholfen und noch heute fristen Millionen ein schattenloses Dasein; sie ziehen ein und aus, ohne Spuren zu hinterlassen; die Organisation der grossen Städte, das rationelle Prinzip der Mietswohnung, das dahin drängt, aus dem Zimmer die Kabine eines Schlafwagens zu machen, helfen mit rührige Architekten thun das ihrige.

Man kann Atmosphäre in einer recht greulichen Wohnung haben; das haben unsere Eltern bewiesen, sie lebten ahnungslos dahin, ohne einen Schimmer der dekorativen Wiedergeburt, mit denen ihre Söhne sich trugen. Und doch wie gemütlich hatten sie's! Wer sehnt sich nicht von der unpersöhnlichen Pracht, von der rationellen Logik einer nach allen Regeln der Kunst modernen Wohnung in unbeobachteten Momenten in die stille Scheusslihkeit der guten, alten Wohnstube zurück!

Wir fangen an, moderne Wohnungen zu bekommen, nun fehlen nur noch die Menschen dazu, Leute, die sich die modernenDinge natürlich zu machen verstehen, die dem Neuen das immer peinliche Neue nehmen, sich in dem Stil stilgerecht bewegen, Leben hineinbringen, Atmosphäre.

Dazu gehört zweierlei, gewisse Eigenschaften der Wohnung wie der Bewohner. Man muss ehrlich genug sein, zu gestehen, dass die Moderne es den Bewohnern nicht immer leicht macht, diese Qualitäten zu äussern. Es giebt in der modernen Dekoration z. B. Dinge, die schlechterdings beziehungslos bleiben müssen, so wenig sind sie aus dem Geist des friedlichen Bewohners gedacht. Sie sind Belege einer mehr oder weniger tiefen Originalität und eignen sich am besten zu dem heutzutage nicht zu übersehenden Zweck, in Kunstzeitschriften abgebildet zu werden. Alles das war und ist recht gut, es lassen sich in dieser Welt die einfachsten Dinge nicht ohne Kampf erreichen, und diese dekorativen Symptome waren die Kriegsflaggen im Kampfe und wenn sie rechtzeitig in die Ecke gestellt werden, soll man sie doppelt schwer mit Lorbeer behängen. Man konnte die Ornamente der alten Zeit nicht mit der kühlen Logik bekämpfen, dass es überhaupt nicht des Ornaments zur Seligkeit bedarf, sondern brauchte neue Ornamente. Das allzu Menschliche bringt es mit sich, dass man dabei den eigentlichen Zweck ins Hintertreffen geraten liess. Wir mussten der Welt Beispiele unserer ungeheuren Originalität geben, um uns nachher um so sicherer ihrer entledigen zu können. Welcher lebenslustige Jüngling ist nicht in der ersten Ballsaison der Versuchung unterlegen, aus seinem Schneider einen Dichter zu machen und berauschende Westen und Fracks zu tragen! – Wenn man in die Jahre kommt und immer noch in diesem heiteren Firelefanz den Ausdruck seiner Persönlichkeit sucht, kann man leicht eine Spur lächerlich werden, auch wenn der innere Habitus noch so Ernst ist. Dann wird sich in dem normal Veranlagten vielmehr ein Drang geltend machen, in solchen Aeusserlichkeiten in der Masse zu verschwinden und die Individualität – wenn man eine hat – keusch unter einer möglichst harmlosen Hülle zu verbergen. Man wird den dringenden Wunsch behalten, tadellos sitzende Kleider zu tragen, aber aus möglichst diskreten Stoffen.

Dieser Wunsch muss sich notgedrungen in die Wohnungsfrage übertragen: mag das Milieu noch so einfach sein, wenn es einem nur sitzt, und die Theorie, ob die Dinge dieser und jener Evolution der modernen Architektur und der modernen Malerei entsprechen, wird sich zu der natürlicheren Frage differenzieren, ob sie dem lieben Ich entsprechen.

Weder VAN DE VELDE, noch ECKMANN, noch PLUMET

oder wer immer hat daran gedacht. Jede Wohnung wurde

ein neuer Stein ihres Wesens, ihre eigene Persöhnlichkeit

legten sie in ihre Zimmer hinein, nicht die ihrer Auftraggeber.

Von diesen sagen ihre Räume nichts, und das bracht nicht

unbedingt darauf zurückzuführen sein, dass ihre Kunden

nichts zu sagn wussten. Sie kannten sie nicht. Wie man von

keinem Schneider einen Anzug ohne Anprobe erwarten kann,

so lässte sich ohne persönliche Beziehung kein harmonisches

Resultat erwarten. Das Massnehmen beschränkt sich bei der

Bestellung der Wohnung auf das Abmessen des Geldbeutels,

allenfalls äussert der Besteller noch seine Wünsche in der

Wahl der Hölzer; in jungen Kulturstaaten, wie Berlin, pflegt

man sich auf das Minimum einer eigenen Meinung zu

beschränken, thut übrigens damit gut und weise.

Die Wohnung, von der ich reden will, hat vor allem

den Vorzug, bewohnt zu sein, d.h. bis zum gewissen Grade

aus den Instinkten heraus geschaffen zu sein, die theoretisch

zwar bei unseren Künstlern vorhanden, aber mehr prinzipiell

allgemein als persöhnlich objektiv betont und von subjektiven

Tendenzen übertroffen werden.

Sie befindet sich in München und wurde von RUDOLF ALEXANDER SCHRÖDER, einem der Herausgeber der von BIERBAUM, HEYMEL und SCHRÖDER gemeinschaftlich redigierten Zeitschrift "Insel", für seine Vetter ALFRED WALTER HEYMEL geschaffen.

Wir haben starke originelle Leute in allen Künsten; was wir noch brauchen in der Poesie, in Malerei, Skulptur, Architektur, ist die Ruhe in der Beherrschung: Geschmack.

Geschmack vor allen Dingen ist das Typische in der HEYMEL'schen Wohnung. Er äussert sich am sichersten in der Tendenz, vor allen Dingen etwas Wohnliches zu schaffen. Und zwar etwas Wohnliches für einen bestimmten Menschen. Die beiden Freunde stehen sich so nahe, dass SCHRÖDER sich nur seinem Wesen zu überlassen brauchte, um seine Aufgabe zu erfüllen. Er that es mit der sicheren Selbstverständlichkeit eines ganz harmonischen Menschen, bei dem das Bedürfnis über das liebe Aeusserliche hinweggeht, der ohne grosse Prätention, aber mit unbewusster Konsequenz seine Art allen Dingen, mit denen er umgeht und bei denen es sich lohnt, aufprägt. Das Merkwürdige an der Wohnung ist der Mangel an allen Dilettantismus. Gerade was den Dilettanten am meisten an der Moderne imponiert, die neue Ornamentik, ist hier mit einer kühlen Sicherheit ausser acht gelassen, die kaum ein Künstler über sich bringt. Die verständige Einsicht, etwas nicht zu können, wozu eben, wenn die Schöpfung orginal sein soll, Specialanlage gehört, diese im allgemeinen so sehr mangelnde Einsicht, die gewöhnlich durch oberflächliche Nachempfindung ersetzt wird, hat hier zu einer fast programmatisch wirkenden Lösung geführt. Man findet nirgends die berühmte belgische Linie, die bereits die Barbierstube im ostpreussischen Dorf schmückt. Es giebt überhaupt kaum Schmuck. Hier und da hat der Künstler die Notwendigkeit empfunden, einen farbigen Fleck hinzubringen, etwas Krauses, etwas Breites, oder Langes; wie sich dieser Fleck detaillierte, war ihm weniger wichtig, er bevorzugte schöne stilisierte Blumen oder begnügte sich mit einem auf ein Minimum reduzierten Kranz von Blättern oder wiederum nahm er ein simples, mathematisches Ornament. Mit der grössten Leichtigkeit ist hier der Satz wieder mal offenbar geworden, dass das Ornament immer nur ein Detail ist und als solches im ganzen zu verschwinden hat. Auf dieses Ganze aber, wie es sich in den Hauptlinien und

Hauptflächen darstellt, verwandte SCHRÖDER alle Sorgfalt. Er hatte mit einer grossen Mietswohnung zu thun, mit dem ganzen Klischeereichtum des modernen Kasernismus. Da gab es keinen Plafond, keine Thür, die bleiben konnte. Er verwandte vor allem grösste Aufmerksamkeit auf die Wände; freilich es stand kein Bauherr hinter ihm, der ihn auf die Vorgänglichkeit der Mietswohnung aufmerksam machte, er durfte den Hauptteil des Budgets gerade auf Dinge verwenden, die mit dem Wechsel der Wohnung unrettbar verloren sind. Gerade darin verrät sich der adlige Sinn sowohl des Auftraggebers wie des Künstlers. Es herrscht eine fast vorsintflutige Gediegenheit in den Räumen, wie man sie nur in den alten Patrizierhäusern unserer Hansastädte findet – in der That stammen SCHRÖDER und HEYMEL aus Bremen. Der wesentlichste Teil des Mobiliars ist eingebaut in die Wände, nicht in komplizierter Form, einfach und praktisch. Vor allem wenig herumstehende Möbel, die Räume haben gerade soviel wie nötig ist, um ihnen Struktur zu geben. Keine Kleinigkeiten, die Sitzgelegenheiten sind ungeheuerlichen Umfangs, Sessel gegen die selbst die englischen Rocking Chairs in Leder wie Zwerge erscheinen; sehr viel Sophas,

42

jedes beinahe eben so tief wie lang, kein sichtbares Holz an den Sitzen, nicht der kleinste, billige Versuch des geschnitzten Schnörkels. Das könnte plump wirken, wenn es nicht gut verteilt wäre. Und gerade darin steckt der grösste Reiz: diese wuchtige Einfachheit entbehrt nicht der Grazie. Vor den riesigen Sophas stehen winzige runde Tischchen, die grossen Schränke sind ausserordentlich geschickt geteilt, die Materialien wechseln mit verblüffender Sicherheit. Da ist zum Beispiel das Schlafzimmer. Das Bett ist ein ungeheures, echt nordisches Bauwerk, ebenso breit wie lang, mit einem kolosalen Himmel ganz aus schwerem Holz. Wäre alles in diesem Zimmer im gleichen Gewicht, würde es unfehlbar erdrückend wirken. Aber diese schwere Fülle des Bettes wird spielend durch den grossen Waschtisch abgelöst, der ebenso einfach wie elegant aus einer auf Messingfüssen ruhenden Marmorplatte besteht. Nicht ohne Keckheit ist diesen reinsten Ausdruck des Modernen zum Trotz zwischen den hohen Bettsäulen des Bettes ein Schmuck verwandt, der im Prinzip gar nicht passen dürfte. Es sind schwere versilberte Kränze, die stark an das Empire gemahnen – und es passt doch, das ist das Kunststück. Ueberhaupt steckt darin ein

Geheimnis der Grazie bei aller Wucht, in der glücklichen Vermischung eines fast pathetisch wirkenden Schmucks und höchst nüchterner Grundformen. Die Engländer haben das schon gezeigt, hier is es mit grösserer Freiheit gelungen. Und dann hilft die Farbe zur Leichtigkeit. Die Wände des Schlafzimmers sind mit blauer Seide bespannt und verlieren sich in einen Fries aus ungebeiztem Mahagoni. Zwischen den Pfeilern des Bettes, an den Fenstern und Thüren hängen schwere gelbseidene Vorhänge, in die in frischen Farben grosse Blumen gestickt sind. Glänzend in der Farbe ist das Esszimmer. Die Wände in zartem Rosa gestrichen, der Fussboden in grauen Fliesen ohne jeden Teppich, dazu wieder Naturmahagoni. Es steht nichts in dem grossen Raum als der gewaltige runde Esstisch und eine Menge grosser, mit Strohsitzen versehener Stühle. Nur an der Wand zum Office zwei schmale Tische. Dazu viel Silber. Die Beleuchtung wird nur von Kerzen gegeben; teils liegt sie an den Wänden in einfachen versilberten Leuchtern, teils auf dem Tisch in niedrigen Kandelabern. In diesem Zimmer ist auch strenge Stilistik; das von dem Künstler bevorzugte einfache Tulpenmuster findet sich überall, in dem Damast, dem Silberbesteck u.s.w. Der gedeckte Tisch bei HEYMEL ist ein kleines Wunder von Geschmack in kostbarer Einfachheit. Das Silberbesteck, das von dem Worpsweder VOGELER sehr geschmackvoll und solid entworfen wurde, mit den famosen, der Knospe der Tulpe entlehnten Griffen, dazu die Tulpengläser von POWELL & SONS, endlich das in seiner Einfachheit verblüffend schöne Porzellan, schneeweiss mit dem bewussten Fries am Rande – alles das wirkt fürstlich zusammen und ist im einzelnen nichts mehr als gut bürgerliche Wohlhabenheit.

Sehr schön ist auch die Diele, ein sehr grosser Raum, der ganz in Spiegelscheiben tapeziert ist, deren feinlinige mathematische Teilung die Flächen kaum merkbar belebt. Hier herrscht dunkle, fast mystische Stille; nichts wie diese geteilten Spiegel, die grossen Sophas mit den winzigen Tischen davor, der enorme Kamin giebt einen ganz bestimmten würdigen Character. Abends wenn die Scheite im Kamin brennen und allein das Licht geben, wird es gemütlich, man rückt den Sessel um den Kamin und vergisst Ort und Zeit, ein Idealraum zum Träumen!

Von der Diele geht es in das Bureau der *Insel*, einen einfach und praktisch eingerichteten Arbeitsraum, und in die Perle des Ganzen, den grossen Salon. Hier ist immer wieder mit einfachsten Mitteln sehr viel mehr gewagt worden. Die Hölzer sind weiss lackiert mit - geschnitzten mattgrün und roten Rosen. Es ist das denkbar Süsseste, und eingefeischte Moderne werden mir nicht glauben, dass es trotzdem nicht süsslich wirkt. Die Decke, von der in zwei grossen konzentrischen Vierecken angeordnet, gegen hundert elektrische Lampen mit einfachen Silberschirm an den Kordeln hängen, ist wieder mit den süssesten Rosenguirlanden dekoriert. An den Wänden graue ins Mattlila fallende Seide; kostbare, schwerseidene Vorhänge derselben Farbe, prunkvoll mit weissen Rosen bestickt, bekleiden Thüren und Fenster, zwischen denen sich grosse Konsolspiegel erheben. Diese Vorhänge sind köstlich. Sie laufen in aufgebauschte Rüschen aus, unter denen mehrfache weisse Unterbehänge hervorschauen. Man glaubt, hinter jedem Vorhang das schlanke Füsschen einer Colombine versteckt und möchte sich als Pierrot in weisse Seide Hüllen. Es ist der Raum der schönen Frauen, wo getanzt und gelacht wird, man kann sich hier nur im Frack unter rauschenden Ballkleidern wohl fühlen.

Typisch für den Geschmack der beiden Freunde ist die tote Staffage dieses Raums. In den Ecken stehen Meissener Vögel in starken, grünen, blauen, rotten Farben. Auf den Tischen, um die sich Sitzmöbel aller nur erdenklichen Formen und Farben gruppieren, findet man die prachtvollen, weissen Porzellantiere von BING & GRÖNDAHL, dazwischen schillernde, altrömische Gläser. Und es ist nicht die Kostbarkeit dieses Nippes, die den Reiz giebt, sondern die lässige, willkürlich scheinende Wahl. Dass diese Dinge kostbar sind, ist fast Zufall; in anderen Räumen ist diese Zusammengehörigkeit zuweilen mit spottbiligen Vasen u. dgl. erreicht, lediglich infolge der Form- und Tonwerte.

Es fehlt der Raum, um auch die anderen Zimmer zu beschreiben, man hat auch nicht davon, man müsste sie sehen. Es giebt noch ein ausserordentlich gediegenes Kupferstichkabinett, in grellstem Blau gehalten und Nussbaum, mit prachtvollen ausserordentlich praktischen Schränken, die im oberen Teil die Schubladen für die Drucke enthalten, während in dem unteren ganz leeren Teil die Tische verschwinden, die man bei der Arbeit herausrollt. Ein Billardsaal und Spielzimmer mit einem sehr suggestiven Barschrank, ein stilles, gemütliches Arbeitszimmer, alles in tadelloser Ausführung, die meist von den Vereinigten Werkstätten besorgt wurde. Es ist überall dasselbe Prinzip guten Geschmacks und gesunden Menschenverstandes. Dieses ist der bleibende Eindruck und er hat springende kulturelle Bedeutung. Hier wurde der Nachweis geliefert, dass es nicht so sehr des A tout prix-Modernismus bedarf, um ein anstuandiges Milieu zu schaffen, als das Prestige der meisten führenden Künstler unserer Bewegung glauben lassen möchte. Sie alle ohne Ausnahme können an dieser einfachen Lösung viel lernen, vor allem das beste der modernen Prinzipien, dass man nicht wenig genug Kunst anwenden kann, um Künstler zu sein. Die Bewegung wird wahrscheinlich und hoffentlich den SCHRÖDER'schen Weg gehen; freilich nicht die Masse. Der Masse wird das schlimmste geschmückte Ding immer mehr imponieren, als das beste schmucklose. Wohl aber ist diese Tendenz von den Führern zu erwarten. Die Wiener fangen schon an,

Loos macht ostentativ in Wien Möbel ohne jedes Ornament und bleibt nicht ohne Einfluss. Moser und Hofmann haben in ihren letzten Möbeln schon eine sehr wohlthuende Strenge. Eckmann in Deutschland hat in seinen besten Sachen demselben Prinzip schon vor langer Zeit gehuldigt, van de Velde scheint sich auch, so weit es seine Eigenart erlaubt, dahin wenden zu wollen, die besseren Architekten Deutschlands und Englands verfolgen mit Eifer denselben Weg, der in England bereits Tradition ist. Es ist der einzige Weg, auf dem ein guter Einfluss auf die Handwerker zu gewinnen ist. Die Kunst wird darin liegen, ihn so sicher vor Trockenheit zu bewahren, wie dies Schröder in diesem Fall gelungen ist.

EPILOGUE

BY MARKUS BREITSCHMID
WITH THE FRIENDLY ADVISE OF HARRY FRANCIS MALLGRAVE

The term *Sachlichkeit* owns two points of historical prominence
in art and architecture. There is a concern of an architectural
realism as *sachliche* art, an architecture that, on one hand,
is bound to the problems of function, comfort, health, and
the inclusion of technical possibilities, and, on the other
hand, refers to milieu, character, locality, and *Stimmung*
(best translated as ambience; sometimes also translated
as atmosphere, but atmosphere relates less to a spatial
Stimmung and more to an exterior atmospheric condition).
This approach to architecture is defined as *Sachlichkeit*. Then
there is also the term *Neue Sachlichkeit*. While *sachliche* art is
proliferated between the last decade of the nineteenth and
first decade of the twentieth centuries, *Neue Sachlichkeit*
belongs almost entirely to the 1920s. *Neue Sachlichkeit* also
speaks of an artistic realism, but what is specifically meant
by it is the true representation of objects as an opposition
against nonrepresentational art. The mimetic vision of *Neue
Sachlichkeit* operates with the 'cold eye' and aims to yield the

intellectual and spiritual conditions of Modern civilization. The aim is the deliberate cultivation of the unsentimental. This is an entirely different perception than the concern about character and atmosphere that were part of *Sachlichkeit* around the turn of the century. Retrospectively, there are two more associations of the term *Sachlichkeit* that one ought to know: There is a *reine* (pure) *Sachlichkeit* that more or less can be equated to the term functionalism, and there is a pseudo-*Sachlichkeit*, whose aim is to symbolize *sachliche* conditions behind a self-imposed historical determinism. The latter cannot be *sachlich* in the sense of the definition it had around 1900 because the *Sachliche* would compromise the semantics of its works of art.

These delineations of the term *Sachlichkeit* lead to the historiography of Modern architecture. It is important to understand that the inclusion of *Sachlichkeit* – now taking into account the meaning of *Sachlichkeit* as it was understood at the turn of the century – undermines the existing paradigm of the historiography of Modernism. Histories on European Modernism that have appeared since the thirties of the previous century point almost exclusively to a crystallization of Modern architecture in Germany and France in the 1920s. Repeatedly it has shown how a few lonely pioneers such as HENDRIK PETRUS BERLAGE, OTTO WAGNER, or FRANK LLOYD WRIGHT have preceded this crystallization. Only the last thirty years has brought some appreciation of figures such as HERMANN MUTHESIUS and PETER BEHRENS. But even with the inclusion of these architects, there persists a problem. There is no compelling course of events to connect MUTHESIUS with WAGNER. The line of development that has been drawn by the architectural historian NIKOLAUS PEVSNER in his landmark study *Pionners of the Modern Movement* of 1936 is symptomatic for almost the entire œuvre of historiography of Modern architecture, namely the attempt to create a single line between WALTER GROPIUS and WILLIAM MORRIS through the window of Art Nouveau.

This lineage is even more problematic if the development of the relations in Germany is studied. It is possible to value the influence of Art Nouveau as more important in Western European developments, such as in France and Belgium, than it was in the Central Europe territories of Germany and Austria. A penetrating look into the growth of architectural Modernism in the German-speaking countries brings to light a situation that is sagerated with various theortical contributions that have their own genealogy, without taking recourse into the developments of Western Europe. If the German situation ought to be explained, it is almost impossible to negate the various contributions and currents that occured during the last three decades of the nineeenth century. It is also important, with respect of a possible history of architecture, that the architectural realism of *Sachlichkeit* comes to existence earlier than Art Nouveau. Moreover, the analysis of the contribution made by the *sachliche* approach suggests that *Sachlichkeit* is a more substantive rational alternative of which Art Nouveau, *Jugendstil,* and *Sezession* are short-lived singular appearances within a more profound and more epochal stream of a *sachliche* approach to architecture, art, and life.

The recent discussion focusing on the Central-European derivation of Modern architecture was sparked by the rediscovery of GOTTFRIED SEMPER. The realization of the importance of SEMPER for the growth of Modern architecture was the initial impetus to revisit the model Morris-Art Nouveau-Gropius. With SEMPER, there is now present a German architect and theoretician in the mid of the nineteenth century who was at least as influential as JOHN RUSKIN in England and EMMANUEL-EUGENE VIOLET-LE-DUC in France. Secondly, and even more important, SEMPER's reflections are retrospectively very Modern, certainly more Modern than anything that his English and French contemporaries advocated. How SEMPER influenced Modern architecture remained a mystery for quite some time, and it was only through the recent scholarly work on WAGNER's œuvre that demonstrated the linkage between SEMPER's thought and theories of the first decade of the twentieth century. It was the newly sparked interest on the subject of German theory at the John Paul Getty Research Institute in Los Angeles in the 1980s and a new evaluation of Historicism that brought to light forgotten and, even in German-speaking places, not recognized figures. From today's perspective we know that Modern German architectural theory was not so much a product of the 1920s but began to take shape even before the death of SEMPER, and took on a mature form in the first decade of the twentieth century. RICHARD LUCAE's *On the Power of Space in the Building Arts* (1869), KARL EMIL OTTO FRITSCH's *How can the art of building again become popular?* (1876), HANS AUER's *The Development of Space in Building Art* (1883), GEORG HEUSER's *Roots of a New Building Style* (1888), AUGUST ENDELL's *Originality and Tradition* (1901), FERDINAND FELDEGG's *Monumentality and Modern Art of Building* (1903), and KARL SCHEFFLER's *A Way to Style* (1903) are an incomplete list of texts of major importance for the formation of Modern architecture largely ignored by Modern historiography. The same can be stated about a number of articles specifically focusing on the subject of *Sachlichkeit*.

While ALFRED LICHTWARK's essay *Sachliche Baukunst* [Realist Architecture] of 1899 emphasizes the interest for the endemic and native in the cause of Modern architecture, there is another important problem that is articulated in the debate focusing on design of Modern life: taste and salubrious common sense. Such are the subjects of the essay *Ein modernes Milieu* [A Modern Milieu] of JULIUS

MEIER-GRAEFE of 1901. MEIER-GRAEFE is best known as one of the eminent European art critics reaching the apex of his influence during the first decade of the twentieth century. Specifically, he made a name for himself as a connoisseur of Impressionism. It is then not much of a stretch of imagination that he also was, for a time during the 1890s, an advocate of HENRY VAN DE VELDE's Art Nouveau, before he turned away from Art Nouveau and *Jugendstil* in 1898. He wrote the essay *Österreich*, published in *Dekorative Kunst*, as one of the very first statements indicating that Vienna had become the center of contemporary architecture. The essay *Ein modernes Milieu*, translated for this volume, is MEIER-GRAEFE's most important contribution in the discipline of architecture. It deals with the apartment of ALFRED WALTER HEYMEL in Munich. More exactly, the essay is a revue of the interior design of the HEYMEL's apartment by the poet RUDOLF ALEXANDER SCHRÖDER with the assistance of the architects MARTIN DÜLFER and PAUL TROOST.

While RICHARD STREITER's contribution *Architektonische Zeitfragen* [Contemporary Architectural Questions] of 1898 is

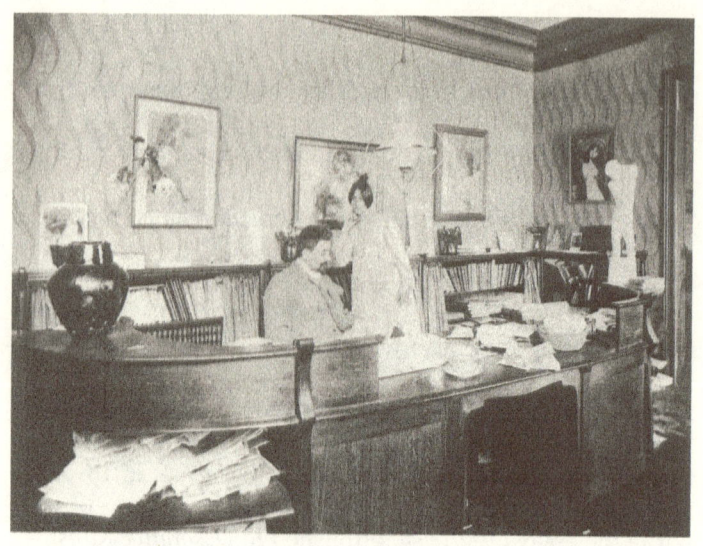

JULIUS MEIER-GRAEFE AT A DESK DESIGNED BY HENRY VAN DE VELDE, PARIS 1897

considered to be the most all-encompassing analysis of the contemporary situation regarding architecture, MEIER-GRAEFE'S article is the most significant from a historical perspective. MEIER-GRAEFE is gushing in his words with respect to the newly found simplicity in the design of the apartment.

MEIER-GRAEFE writes, "Everywhere there is the same principle of good taste and a healthy dose of common sense. This is the abiding impression and it has a salient cultural significance. Here we see that it does not require infinitely profound art or much of a Modernism *a tout prix* to create a suitable milieu, as the prestige of most of the leading artists of our movement would like us to believe. Without exception all of them could learn a lot from this simple solution, especially the best of the modern principles — that one cannot use too little art in order to be an artist."

MEIER-GRAEFE begins his essay with an apology because he used two foreign words in his very short title. Laconically, he states that nothing else came to his mind that would have explained the matter at hand more succinct. The word milieu is interpreted to show that now there really is an apartment in which one can live in. The wording suggests a hint aimed towards the *Jugenstil*-designs of the artist colony at Mathildenhöhe in Darmstadt, in particular the design of PETER BEHRENS for his own house.

MEIER-GRAFE discovers another quality in the Heymel-apartment: the demand that the Modern milieu must be awakend by Modern life; only be means of an authentic Modern life can one achieve an atmosphere, mood, and disposition of actual life.

What the article *Ein modernes Milieu* calls for is that *sachliche* art of building needs the "Lässliche", the casual in the sense of nonchalant, that already was important for STREITER. This approach reminds us of a word of NIETZSCHE: "A work of art, that is an expression of the healthy, can only be borne with three-forths of the power of the creator. On the other hand, if the creator has gone to his utmost boundaries, the work of art will fluster the onlooker and cause anxiety by means of its tension. All good things have something nonchalant about them and lay dispersed like cows on a meadow."[1]

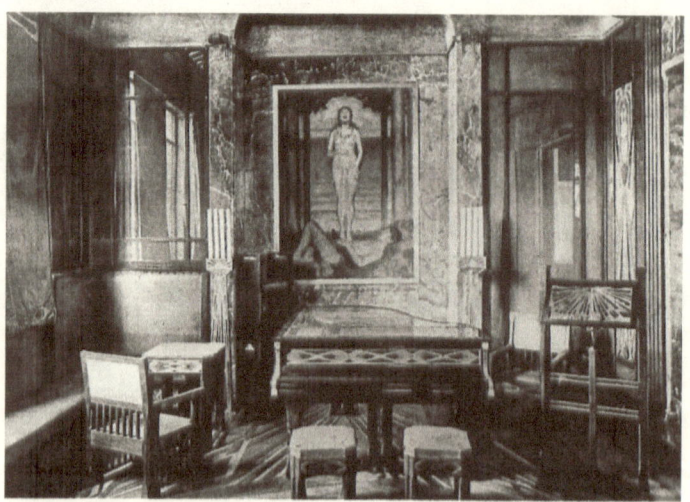

INTERIOR OF HOUSE BEHRENS AT MATHILDENHÖHE-DARMSTADT, 1901. DESIGNED BY PETER BEHRENS

---

[1] Nietzsche, Friedrich. Menschliches, Allzumenschliches II: Vermischte Meinungen und Sprüche # 107 In: Kritische Studienausgabe (Giorgio Colli; Mazzino Montinari, eds.) Volume 2, Berlin, New York: Walter de Gruyter 1988, p. 422.

In the eyes of MEIER-GREAFE, the work of BEHRENS brings to the foreground a new peril to which STREITER has already pointed: the fall into the mechanical. The abstract classicism of BEHRENS is now the pseudo-*Sachlichkeit* that is described earlier in this epilogue. The pseudo-*Sachlichkeit* has no place for life on this earth but strives towards truth with theosophical absolutism. In the case of the early twentieth century this meant the abstract symbolization of the machine-like which eventually lead to the machine-style. As *Sachlichkeit* changed into this so-called new form, MEIER-GRAEFE was at the forefront of critizising this shift into the absolute. He contended that this new trend is not a unification of beauty and need, form and function, art

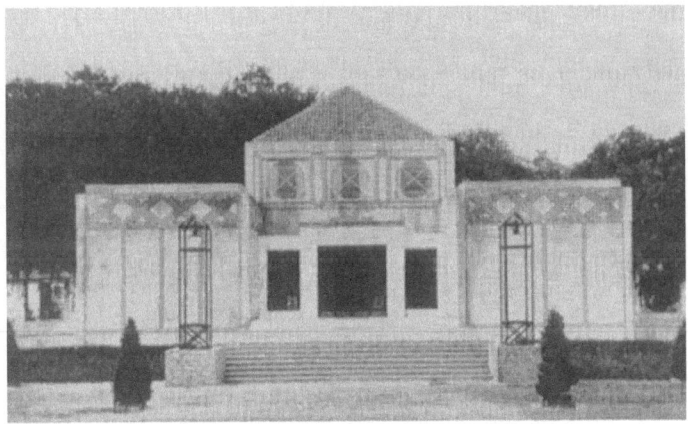

EXHIBITION PAVILION, OLDENBURG, 1905. DESIGNED BY PETER BEHRENS.

and life, but identified one with the other. He argues, that the aesthetic did not conquer life but that a sort of Hegelian historical-materialist determinism has absorbed art. For MEIER-GRAEFE, the new art of pseudo-*Sachlichkeit,* as well as the *Neue Sachlichkeit* that followed about a decade later, appears as a reduction and as an impoverishment of the architectural production. The world of art and architecture, according to MEIER-GRAEFE, enters a phase of ptochocracy. There is no need for that. MEIER-GRAEFE favors SCHRÖDER and ADOLF LOOS specifically because their work always remained splendorous [*"prächtig"],* luxurious, and valuable despite its logic of construction, its simple language of straight lines, its simple massing, and its quiet surfaces. When MEIER-GRAEFE describes the furnishings of the apartment of HEYMEL, for example the arrangment of the armchairs, one is indeed reminded of NIETZSCHE'S "cows on the meadow"; certainly we do not sense a "tension" as in the interior of BEHRENS in Darmstadt.

The "tension" discovered in the Modern art production is what WILHELM WORRINGER described as the "enormous wanting for reposefulness" of the Northern-

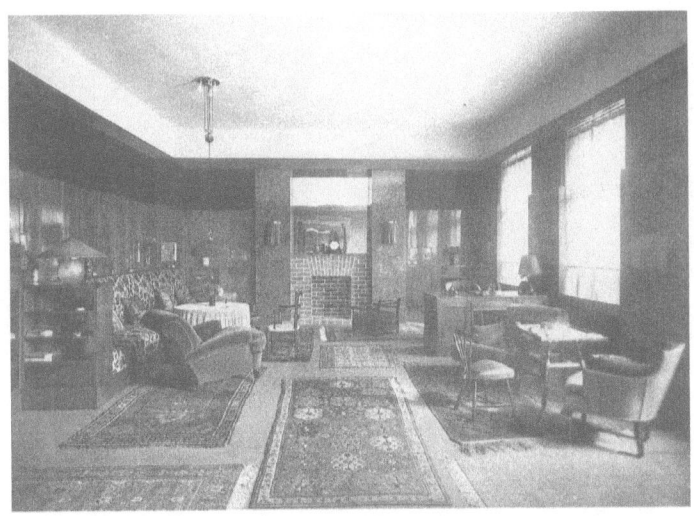

SITTING ROOM OF VOGL APARTMENT, PILSEN-BOHEMIA, 1929. DESIGNED BY ADOLF LOOS.

European man.[2] This man is a man of an idealistic kingdom-come, entirely different from the man who complaisantly craves for the admiration of the here and now. The man who is living in the here and now loves to empathize with the world, while the Modern man of the early twentieth century always places everything into the abstract and absolute depth of space.[3] WORRINGER confirms MEIER-GRAEFE and STREITER: abstraction stands above empathy for the democratic men of the machine age, his sense of beauty lies "in the realm of the

[2] Worringer, Wilhelm. Abstraktion und Einfühlung. Ein Beitrag zur Stil-psychologie. München: Fundus [1908] 1996, p. 50.

[3] Wyss, Beat. Der Wille zur Kunst. Zur ästhetischen Mentalität der Moderne. Köln: Dumont 1997, p. 248.

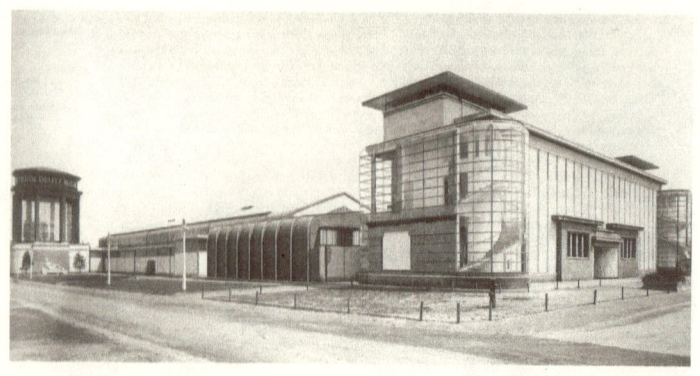

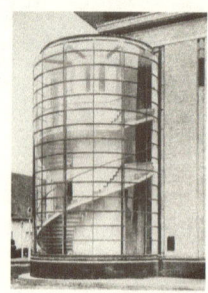

Deutz Machine Factory for the *Werkbund* Exhibition, Cologne, 1914. Designed by Walter Gropius and Adolf Meyer

life-negating anorganic, in the crystalline, generally speaking, in all abstract lawfulness and necessity ... life as such is sensed as a disturbance of the aesthetic pleasure."[4]

For this reason, the simple line of Behrens or Gropius is not the same simple line as the one of Schröder or Loos. The simple line and its formations according to geometric laws offers for Behrens and Gropius "the biggest possibility for bliss ... because here the last residue of life-

---

[4] Worringer. Op. Cit. p. 37.

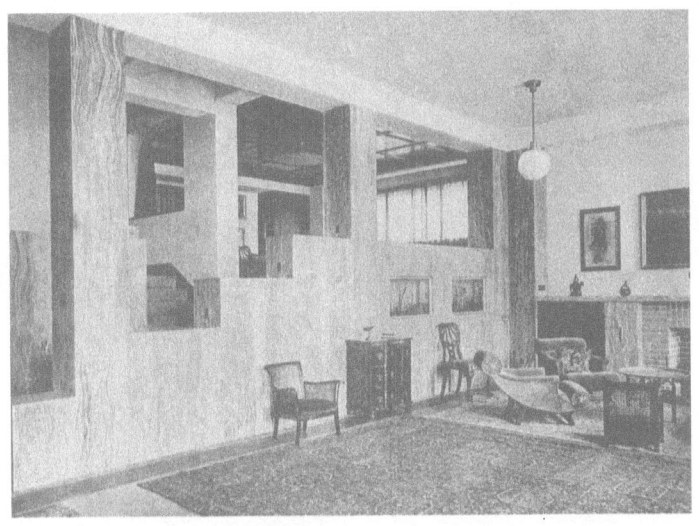

SITTING ROOM AT HOUSE MÜLLER, PRAGUE, 1928-30. DESIGNED BY ADOLF LOOS.

coherence and life-reliance is obliterated, here the highest

abstract form, the purest abstraction is attained; here exists

the law, necessity where otherwise the arbitrariness of the

organic predominates."[5]   MEIER-GRAEFE does not see the

future of Modern art in the realm of the transcendence, and

he is probably not incorrect when he states that the body of

work of BEHRENS presents the implementation of empathy

into mechanization. SCHRÖDER, on the other hand, did not

succumb to this hazard. He achieved a happy solution

between an overly decorated and overly personal expression

on one side, and the cold, sterile, and sometimes mystically

---

[5]   Worringer. Ibid., p. 55.

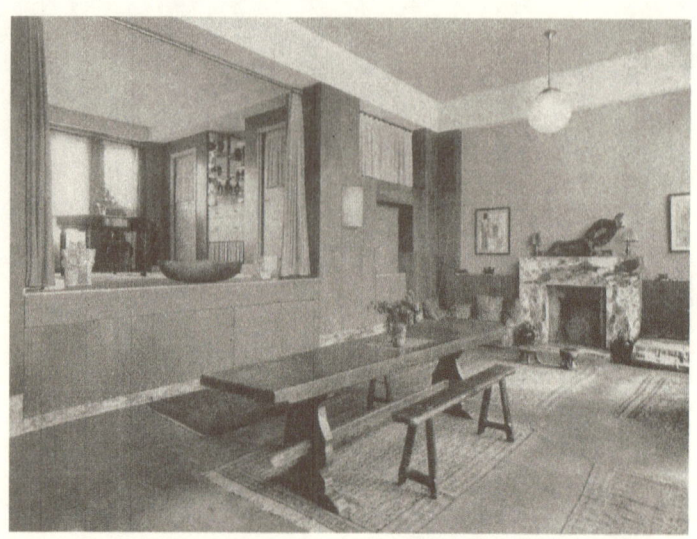

SITTING ROOM AND RAISED DINING ROOM AT HOUSE TZARA, PARIS, 1925-26. DESIGNED BY ADOLF LOOS.

elevated symbolic art on the other side. MEIER-GRAEFE did not give a name to this agenda but an important program for the Modern movement was written. As already mentioned above, MUTHESIUS took up the same subject a few months after the publication of MEIER-GRAEFE's *Ein modernes Milieu*. From his own Prussian perspective, MUTHESIUS synthesized the results of the endemic and native-oriented LICHTWARK with the formulations of the cosmopolitan approach of WAGNER under the mediation of the texts of STREITER and MEIER-GRAEFE. It was thus MUTHESIUS who became the well-known propagator of the debate of architectural *Sachlichkeit*.

Julius Meier-Graefe was born in Pesitza in the Banat (a region today belonging to Hungary and Romania) that was part of the Habsburg Empire on June 10 in 1867. His father Edward Meier, an engineer, was very important in introducing iron-processing techniques to Germany and an important figure in the growth of the industry in the Rhineland, Westphalia, and Silesia. The mother, Maria Graefe, died at Julius's birth. Julius added the name Graefe to honor his mother. Julius spent his first years in Westphalia before his family moved to Upper Silesia in 1879 where Julius took his *Abitur* and is encouraged by his father to become an engineer. In 1888, he begins his studies at the University of Munich but becomes interested in painting and makes a first trip to Paris where he sees the world's fair. In 1890, he attends lectures by Grimm, Lazarus, Treitschke, and Simmel at the University of Berlin, but left the university without obtaining a degree. He begins to write novels, becomes involved with the Berlin bohemia, and, at that point, starts his career as an art critic. While mainly living either in Berlin,

Munich, or Paris, he travels all over Europe and becomes one of the leading *commis voyageur* of the European art world with personal contacts to the elite of artists, museum directors, art historians, and critics. In 1894, he founds, with RICHARD DEHMEL and OTTO JULIUS BIERBAUM, the art association PAN. Although a founder of the association, MEIER-GRAEFE is released as the art editor in 1895 because of pressure by ALFRED LICHTWARK and EBERHARD VON BODENHAUSEN and their impression that MEIER-GRAEFE's interests were a further example of an abstract universal approach to culture and an Europeanism infiltrating what they had hoped would be a specifically German magazine. MEIER-GRAEFE becomes a writer for the journals *Das Atelier* and *Die Zukunft*. In 1897, he founds the magazine *Dekorative Kunst*. It is during that time that MEIER-GRAEFE writes on issues concerning architecture and the decorative arts. Of particular interest in the context of this book is an essay entitled *Österreich* where he points to the achievements of Viennese architecture and furniture design. While having been close to the *Jugenstil* for several years and writing from a VAN DE VELDE desk, MEIER-GRAEFE had already begun reassessing that movement in 1899. He criticized architects and artists all over Europe for copying VAN DE VELDE'S excessive concern for his uniqueness or their indulgence in an *Orginalitätsmanie* that precludes the creation of a unified culture and style. Then, in 1901, MEIER-GRAEFE writes the essay *Ein modernes Milieu,* one of the classics of early *Sachlichkeit.* In 1904, MEIER-GRAEFE publishes his most significant larger treatise *Entwicklungsgeschichte der modernen Kunst* [Modern Art: Being a Contribution to a New System of Aesthetics, translated in 1908] - in many regards a more expansive version of his essay *Beitrag zu einer modernen Ästhetik* of 1899 - that essentially is the first history of Modern art. MEIER-GRAEFE has most often been characterized as an impressionist art critic and there is scarcely another person in Europe who was so fully aware of the entire development in France and elsewhere at that time. In fact, MEIER-GRAEFE was responsible for the first comprehensive exhibition of Impressionist art to be held in the German-speaking world, at the Vienna *Sezession* building in 1903. But his conception of Impressionism was not an orthodox one of the time and he did not believe it to be the last phase of naturalism, a passive recording of nature free of tradition. He becomes the center of the famous 'Berlin Circle' that included TILLA DURIEUX, RAINER

71

Maria Rilke, Hugo von Hofmannsthal, Richard Dehmel, and Max Reinhardt. Meier-Graefe published powerful polemical tracts on the two most revered Germanic artists *(Der Fall Böcklin* of 1905 and *Der junge Menzel: Ein Problem der Kunstökonomie Deutschlands* of 1906). The famous *Jahrhundertausstellung* held in the *Nationalgalerie* Berlin on nineteenth-century German painting in 1906 was largely due to the initiative of Meier-Graefe. In 1905, Meier-Graefe wrote his last article on architecture. The article deals with the abstracted architectural classicism of Peter Behrens, which appeared to him to be the most promising direction for the future of architecture and design. A few years later as German architecture launched into what Meier-Graefe conceived as *Maschinenstil,* an aesthetics based on the machine metaphor, Meier-Graefe was unwilling to support this direction spearheaded by Walter Gropius. This is the decade when Meier-Graefe, who held the most developed position in respect to the late-nineteenth century art, became a force that was viewed as conservative within the German discussion on art. Advanced sensibility would from now on see expression and clear articulation of bare material function as beauty. Even before the beginning of the first World War,

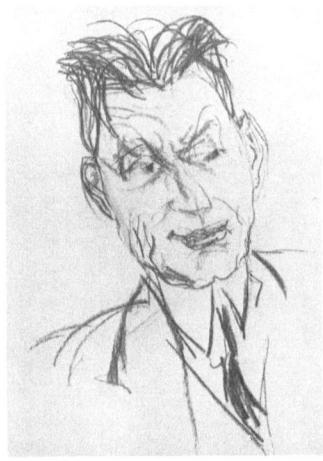

RUDOLF GROSSMANN, PORTRAIT OF
JULIUS MEIER-GRAFE, 1925

MEIER-GRAEFE was no longer regarded as a forward-looking
critic. This valuation was supported by MEIER-GRAEFE'S interest
in the work of the painter HANS VON MARÉES and for the *Marées-
Gesellschaft* after 1917. MEIER-GRAEFE was a volunteer to drive
Red Cross ambulances during the war. In 1915, he got captured
and imprisoned in Omsk, Sibira, for nine months. In 1921, he
moves into a house designed by architect HERMANN MUTHESIUS
in Berlin. MEIER-GRAEFE relocates to France for health reasons
in 1930 and remains active as a critic until his death on June 5,
1935 in Vevey, Switzerland.

SELECTED WRITINGS WITH AN EMPHASIS ON ARCHITECTURE
OR ARCHITECTS BY JULIUS MEIER-GREAFE

MONOGRAPH:

Die Weltausstellung in Paris. Mit zahlreichen photographischen Beilagen und Plänen [The World's Fair in Paris. With Numerous Photographic Illustrations and Drawings], edited by J. Meier-Graefe; F. Kruger. Contains three essys by J. Meier-Graefe: "Architektur" [Architecture], "Malerei-Skulptur" [Painting-Sculpture], "Gewerbe" [Art & Crafts]. Paris-Leipzig 1900

ARTICLES IN JOURNAL *DEKORATIVE KUNST:*

1898:
"Österreich"
"C.V.A. Voysey"
"Peter Behrens"

1899:
"Französische Architektur"
"Henry van de Velde"
"Darmstadt"
"Amerikanische Architektur"

1900:
"Peter Behrens"
"V[ıctor] Horta"

1901:
"Das Moderne Milieu"

1905:
"Peter Behrens, Düsseldorf"

ARTICLES IN OTHER JOURNALS:

"Wie wir wohnen wollen", *Die Woche,* No. 2/41, 1900
"Die Architecktur auf der Weltausstellung", *Die Zukunft,* No. 8/31, 1900
"Modernes Milieu", *Die Kunst,* 1901
"Peter Behrens, Düsseldorf", *Kunst für alle,* Volume 12, 1905

HARRY FRANCIS MALLGRAVE is a trained architect and architectural historian from the United States of America. He obtained his doctorate at the University of Pennsylvania. One of the foremost architectural historians of his generation, he currently is teaching at the Illinois Institute of Technology in Chicago.

MARKUS BREITSCHMID is a trained architect and architectural historian from Switzerland. He obtained his doctorate at the Technische Universität Berlin. He currently is teaching at Virginia Polytechnic Institute & State University in Blacksburg.

TEXTS ON ARCHITECTURE AND ART
A SERIES OF VIRGINIA TECH ARCHITECTURE PUBLICATIONS
MARKUS BREITSCHMID, EDITOR OF SERIES

In Print:

Julius Meier-Graefe. A Modern Milieu [1901] 2007
Edited and with an Epilogue by Markus Breitschmid
Translation by Harry Francis Mallgrave & Markus Breitschmid
ISBN 978-0-9794296-0-6

In Preparation:

Alfred Lichtwark. Realist Architecture [1899]
Edited by Markus Breitschmid
Translation by Harry Francis Mallgrave & Markus Breitschmid

Eduard van der Nüll. Suggestion on the Skillful Relation of
Ornament to Untreated Form [1845]
Edited and with an Epilogue by Hans Rott
Translation by Hans Rott

Hermann Muthesius. New Ornament and New Art [1901]
Edited by Markus Breitschmid
Translation by Harry Francis Mallgrave & Markus Breitschmid

Fritz Schumacher. Style and Fashion [1889, 1902]
Edited by Markus Breitschmid
Translation by Harry Francis Mallgrave & Markus Breitschmid

Virginia Tech Architecture Publications
Blacksburg, Virginia 24061-0205
United States of America
Phone: +1-540-231-5383
www.archdesign.vt.edu